D0235975

[easy**sushi**]

RYLAND
PETERS
& SMALL

London New York

easysushi

emi kazuko
photography by peter cassidy

First published in Great Britain in 2000 by **Ryland Peters & Small**,
Cavendish House, 51–55 Mortimer Street, London W1N 7TD

10 9 8 7 6 5 4 3 2 1

Printed and bound in China by Toppan Printing Co.

ISBN 1 84172 075 5

A CIP record for this book is available from the British Library.

Author's Acknowledgements

I would like to thank those Japanese sushi chefs, past and present,
without whose devotion and hard work sushi would never have become
such a phenomenon the world over. My special thanks goes to my dear
friend Katsuko Hirose whose unceasing support and encouragement from
Japan have given me so much strength over the years. I would also like
to thank Elsa Petersen-Schepelern, for painstakingly editing this book.

Notes

All spoon measurements are level unless otherwise noted.
Uncooked or partly cooked eggs should not be served to the very old or frail,
the very young or to pregnant women.
Specialist Japanese ingredients are available in larger supermarkets, Asian
markets and through mail order sources [page 63].

Dedication

To my late parents who provided me with a good foundation in life and food.

Designer ▸ sailesh patel. **Senior Designer** ▸ louise leffler.

Commissiioning Editor ▸ elsa petersen-schepelern. **Editor** ▸ maddalena bastianelli.

Production ▸ patricia harrington. **Art Director** ▸ gabriella le grazie. **Publishing Director** ▸ alison starling.

Food Stylist ▸ emi kazuko. **Cooking Assistant** ▸ yasuko fukuoka. **Stylist** ▸ wei tang. **Photographer's Assistant** ▸ christian barnett.

contents

introduction

Sushi, for many in the West a synonym for Japanese food, is a general term for all dishes using *sumeshi* [vinegared rice] in combination with other ingredients, mainly raw fish. However, sushi began life not in Japan, but in ancient South-east Asia as a method for preserving fresh fish in steamed rice with salt.

Sushi was developed in its present form, based on vinegared rice, in the nineteenth century and flourished on street stalls in Edo, now Tokyo. It was the 'fast food' of the time — and in many ways it still is. Many of my childhood memories are associated with my mother's sushi as a special lunch for school outings, sports days and theatres.

There are four main types:

1 Rice rolled in sun-dried nori seaweed with ingredients in the centre [page 12], known as *maki-zushi* or *norimaki*.

2 Rice pressed in a mould, topped with cured or salted fish [page 31], known as *oshi-zushi* or *bo-zushi*.

3 'Fingers' of rice with a slice of fish, seafood or omelette on top [page 46], known as *nigiri-zushi*.

4 Bowls of rice with other ingredients mixed through or arranged on top [page 50], known as *chirashi-zushi*.

All are easy to make at home as shown in this book, though *nigiri* is normally eaten at restaurants as it requires trained hands to mould rice to the right hardness so that the whole piece can be picked up easily yet still loosen once in the mouth. In *Easy Sushi*, I have introduced some new ideas so you will be be able to have fun making sushi, using readily available ingredients as well as more authentic kinds. Many ingredients are now available in larger supermarkets and specialist food stores.

The key to success in handling rice is to treat it like a child: be gentle but firm with authority. Do not be put off at your first attempt; you need patience just as with children, and practice really does make perfect.

Sushi is ideal for parties too; rolled sushi *[norimaki]* and pressed sushi *[oshi-zushi]* can be made the day before and kept [at room temperature] until ready to serve. The lunchbox sushi mixture *[chirashi]* can also be prepared in advance and mixed with the other ingredients just before serving. Many sushi combinations are also suitable for vegetarians. Try sushi: you'll find it's easy.

ingredients

Japanese ingredients are becoming more widely available in supermarkets and specialist food stores, but can certainly be found in Asian markets. This directory will help you identify them.

shoyu
[Japanese soy sauce]

mirin
[Japanese sweet rice wine, for cooking only]

su
[Japanese rice vinegar]

sake
[Japanese rice wine]

nori
[sheets of dried seaweed]

kanpyo
[dried gourd ribbons]

kombu
[dried kelp for cooking rice]

white sesame seeds

black sesame seeds

renkon, sliced
[lotus root]

shiso leaf
[Japanese herb, also known as perilla]

abura-age
[fried bean curd]

takuan
[pickled daikon radish]

fresh ginger

Japanese short-grained rice

umeboshi
[pickled red plums]

ready-made pickled ginger

wasabi paste
[also available as powder in tins]

shiitake
[dried mushrooms, also available fresh]

Sushi is a general term for all food with 'sumeshi', or vinegared rice. Remember — sushi should never be put in the fridge [it will go hard]. The vinegar will help preserve it for a few days if kept, wrapped, in a cool place, such as a shady window sill. To make sushi rice, boil 15 per cent more water than rice. So use 1 cup rice to 1 cup plus just over 1 tablespoon water.

vinegared rice sumeshi

400 ml Japanese rice*
1 piece of dried kelp [*kombu*],
    5 cm square, for flavouring
    [optional]
3 tablespoons Japanese rice
    vinegar
2½ tablespoons sugar
2 teaspoons sea salt

Makes 1 litre

* Rice should always be
    measured by volume,
    not weight.

1   Put the rice in a large bowl and wash it thoroughly, changing the water several times, until the water is clear. Drain and leave in the strainer for 1 hour. If short of time, soak the rice in clear cold water for 10–15 minutes, then drain.

2   Transfer to a deep, heavy-based saucepan, add 460 ml water and a piece of dried kelp [*kombu*], if using. Cover and bring to the boil over a high heat, about 5 minutes. Discard the kelp.

3   Lower the heat and simmer, covered, for about 10 minutes, or until all the water has been absorbed. Do not lift the lid. Remove from the heat and leave, still covered, for about 10–15 minutes.

4   Mix the rice vinegar, sugar and salt in a small jug or bowl and stir until dissolved.

5   Transfer the cooked rice to a large, shallow dish or *handai* [Japanese wooden *sumeshi* tub]. Sprinkle generously with the vinegar dressing.

6   Using a wooden spatula, fold the vinegar dressing into the rice. Do not stir. While folding, cool the rice quickly using a fan. Let the rice cool to body temperature before using to make sushi.

Wonderful party food, nori rolls [*norimaki*] are probably the best-known sushi of all. A sheet of nori seaweed is spread with sushi rice, a line of filling put down the middle, then the sheet is rolled up into a cylinder. The cylinder is cut into sections before serving. All ingredients are sold in Asian shops and larger supermarkets.

simple rolled sushi norimaki

¾ quantity vinegared rice
[page 11]

Hand vinegar:
**4 tablespoons Japanese rice
vinegar**
250 ml water

For rolling:
**18 cm piece cucumber,
unpeeled**
3 sheets nori seaweed
wasabi paste or powder

To serve:
pickled ginger
extra wasabi paste
Japanese soy sauce *[shoyu]*

a sushi rolling mat [makisu]

Makes 6 rolls
[36 pieces]

1   Prepare the vinegared rice *[sumeshi]* as in the previous recipe. Mix the hand vinegar ingredients in a small bowl and set aside.

2   To prepare the cucumber, cut into quarters lengthways, then cut out the seeds and cut the remainder, lengthways, into 1 cm square matchstick lengths. You need 6 strips, each with some green skin.

3   Just before assembling, pass the nori over a very low gas flame or hotplate, just for a few seconds to make it crisp and bring out the flavour. Cut each sheet in half crossways.

4   Assemble the sushi according to the method on the following pages.

5   Cut each roll into 6 pieces, as shown on page 14–15.

6   Arrange on a serving plate and serve with pickled ginger, a little pile of wasabi paste and a dish of Japanese soy sauce.

Make the vinegared rice *[sumeshi]*, prepare and assemble the ingredients, then dip your hands in the bowl of hand vinegar.

1 Put a sushi rolling mat *[makisu]* on your work surface, then put half a sheet of toasted nori seaweed on top. Take a handful of the rice [2–3 heaped tablespoons] in your hands and make into a log shape. Put the rice in the centre of the nori.

2 Using your fingers, spread it evenly all over, leaving about 1.5-cm margin on the far side. [The rice will stick to your hands, so dip them in the hand vinegar first.]

3 Take a small dot of wasabi paste on the end of your finger and draw a line down the middle across the rice, leaving a light green shadow on top of the rice [not too much – wasabi is very hot!]

4   Arrange 1 strip of cucumber across the rice, on top of the wasabi.

5   Pick up the mat from the near side and keep the cucumber in the centre.

6   Roll the mat over to meet the other side so that the rice stays inside the nori.

7   Lift the top edge of the mat. Press and roll the cylinder slightly. The join should be underneath so it will stick well [it sticks together because of the moisture in the rice]. Remove the cylinder from the mat and put, join side down, in a covered flat container while you make the remaining rolls.

8   Cut each roll in half, then each half into 3, making 6 pieces. Arrange on a serving plate and serve with pickled ginger, a little pile of wasabi paste and a dish of Japanese soy sauce.

Other ingredients traditionally used for rolled sushi in Japan include *kanpyo* [dried gourd ribbons], tuna with spring onion, *natto* [steamed fermented soy beans] chilli-marinated cod's roe and salted plum [*umeboshi*] with shiso herb. You can also make variations using ingredients more readily available in the West.

rolled sushi variations

¾ quantity vinegared rice
   [page 11]
3 sheets nori seaweed

Hand vinegar:
4 tablespoons Japanese
   rice vinegar
250 ml water

Filling:
100 g fresh salmon,
   skinned
6 cm pickled daikon
   [takuan], cut lengthways
   into 1 cm square sticks
4–6 fresh shiso leaves or
   6–8 basil leaves
2 small red salted plums
   [umeboshi], pitted and
   torn in pieces
wasabi paste

To serve:
pickled ginger
extra wasabi paste
Japanese soy sauce [shoyu]

*a sushi rolling mat
   [makisu]*

Makes 36 pieces

1   Make the vinegared rice [sumeshi] following the recipe on page 11. Mix the hand vinegar ingredients in a small bowl.

2   Cut the piece of salmon into 1 cm square sticks. To make a salmon sushi, follow the method on the previous page, using a row of salmon strips instead of cucumber. [Enough to make 2 rolls.]

3   To make a pickled daikon sushi, follow the method on the previous page, using 3 strips of pickled daikon [takuan] in a row instead of cucumber, and omitting the wasabi paste. [Enough to make 2 rolls.]

4   To make the pickled plum sushi, follow the method on the previous page, using the shiso or basil leaves and the pieces of plum. [Enough to make 2 rolls.]

5   Cut each roll into 6 pieces, then arrange on a plate and serve with pickled ginger, a mound of wasabi paste and a dish of soy sauce.

Variation:
You can also leave the salmon fillet whole, then lightly grill it for about 2 minutes on each side. Cool, put in a bowl, flake with a fork, then stir in 2 finely chopped spring onions. Mix in 2 teaspoons mayonnaise, salt and pepper, then proceed as in the main recipe.

big sushi rolls futomaki

Thick nori rolls normally contain 5 ingredients with contrasting colours, all wrapped up in a whole sheet of nori. A little difficult to eat, but a beautiful party dish.

1 quantity vinegared rice [page 11]
3 sheets nori seaweed

Hand vinegar:
4 tablespoons Japanese rice vinegar
250 ml water

Fillings:
9–12 uncooked king prawn tails, unpeeled
4 eggs
4 tablespoons sugar
250 g spinach
3½ tablespoons Japanese soy sauce [shoyu]
20 g dried gourd [kanpyo] or 1 carrot,
   cut into 5 mm square shreds
5–6 dried shiitake [mushrooms]
1 tablespoon mirin or sweet sherry
salt

To serve:
pickled ginger
Japanese soy sauce [shoyu]

a sushi rolling mat [makisu]

Makes 3 rolls [24 pieces]

1   Make the vinegared rice following the recipe on page 11. Mix the hand vinegar ingredients in a small bowl and set aside.

2   Skewer a cocktail stick through each prawn from head to tail to prevent curling while cooking. Blanch in boiling water for 3 minutes until firm and pink. Immediately plunge into cold water and drain. Remove and discard the cocktail sticks, shells and dark back vein.

3   Using the eggs, 2 tablespoons of the sugar and a pinch of salt, make an omelette following the method on page 60. Let cool, then cut lengthways into 1 cm square sticks.

4   Blanch the spinach in lightly salted water for 1 minute. Plunge into cold water. Drain and pat dry with kitchen paper. Sprinkle with 2 teaspoons soy sauce and set aside.

5   If using kanpyo, rub it with salt and a little water, then soak in water for 10 minutes and drain. Cut into 20 cm lengths. Soak the shiitake in warm water for 30 minutes, then drain, retaining the soaking water. Cut the shiitake into 5 cm strips. Put 250 ml of the soaking liquid in a small saucepan with 3 tablespoons soy sauce, 2 tablespoons of the sugar and the mirin or sherry. Bring to the boil. Add the kanpyo or carrot shreds and shiitake strips. Simmer over a low heat for 15 minutes. Let cool in the liquid and set aside.

6   Toast the nori and put, crossways, one whole sheet at a time, on a sushi rolling mat, following the method on page 16. Dip your hands in the hand vinegar. Take one sixth of the rice and squeeze it between your hands into a firm ball. Put the rice ball on one side of the nori sheet in the centre and, using wet fingers, spread evenly over the half side of nori, leaving about 3 cm margin on the far side. Repeat this once more to fill the other half. The rice layer should be fairly thick – add extra rice if necessary.

7   Arrange 3–4 prawns in a row across the rice about 5 cm from the front edge. Add a row of omelette strips and a row of spinach on top of the prawns. Add a row of kanpyo or carrot and a row of shiitake on top, so that all 5 ingredients are piled in the centre of the rice, like logs of timber. Each roll should use one-third of each ingredient.

8   Pick up the mat from the near side and, keeping all the ingredients in the centre, roll the mat following the method on page 14–15. Remove the mat and put the roll on a plate, join-side down. Repeat to make 2 more rolls.

9   Cut each roll into 8 and serve with little dishes of soy sauce and pickled ginger.

This battleship-shaped version of *nigiri-zushi* has a ribbon of nori seaweed wrapped vertically around the rice, with added toppings such as *ikura* [salmon caviar] and sea urchin. This recipe includes Western variations using crabmeat.

battleship rolls
gunkanmaki

½ quantity vinegared rice [page 11]
1½ sheets nori seaweed

Hand vinegar:
4 tablespoons vinegar
250 ml water

Toppings:
8–12 tablespoons crabmeat*
about 1 teaspoon sake
2 teaspoons wasabi paste or powder
4–6 tablespoons salmon caviar *[ikura]*
   or red lumpfish caviar
12 pickled caperberries or capers

To serve:
pickled ginger
Japanese soy sauce *[shoyu]*

Makes 12

Use white and brown crabmeat from your fishmonger, or good-quality canned crab.

1   Make the vinegared rice *[sumeshi]* following the method on page 11. Mix the hand vinegar ingredients in a small bowl.

2   Put the crabmeat in a small plate and sprinkle with a little sake. If using wasabi powder, mix 1–2 teaspoons powder in an egg cup with 1–2 teaspoons water to make a clay-like consistency. Turn it upside down and set aside to prevent it drying.

3   Cut the whole sheet of nori crossways into 8 ribbons, 18 x 2.5 cm, and the ½ sheet into 4, making 12 ribbons in total.

4   Dip your hands in the vinegar mixture, then take about 1–2 tablespoons rice in one hand and squeeze it into a rectangular mound about 5 x 2 x 3 cm high. Wrap a nori ribbon around it, overlapping about 2 cm at the end. Glue it together with a grain of vinegared rice. Put 2 teaspoons caviar and a few pickled caperberries or capers on top. Repeat to make 3 more rolls with caviar, 4 with crabmeat topped with a little salmon caviar and 4 with crabmeat, with a tiny dot of wasabi on top.

5   Arrange on a platter, and serve with the pickled ginger and a small dish of soy sauce as party food. If making individual servings, serve the soy sauce in small, separate dishes.

½ quantity vinegared rice
   [page 11]
4 small lollo rosso leaves
4 butter lettuce leaves
4 small iceberg lettuce leaves
Japanese soy sauce [shoyu],
   to serve

Hand vinegar:
4 tablespoons Japanese rice
   vinegar
250 ml water

Toppings:
75 g smoked haddock
1 bay leaf
1 teaspoon sugar
75 g smoked salmon, finely
   chopped
1 tablespoon lemon juice
4–6 tablespoons black
   lumpfish caviar
1 tablespoon caperberries or
   capers, drained

Makes 12

1   Make the vinegared rice [sumeshi] following the method on page 11. Mix the hand vinegar ingredients in a small bowl and set aside.

2   Put the haddock and bay leaf in a saucepan, cover with boiling water, return to the boil, then simmer for 5 minutes or until cooked. Drain well. Remove and discard the skin and all the small bones. Put in a bowl and flake finely with a fork. Stir in the sugar and let cool.

3   Sprinkle the smoked salmon with lemon juice.

4   Cut a 3 cm wide strip crossways from the top of the lollo rosso and butter lettuce leaves. Make a small cup, 7 cm diameter, from the inner iceberg leaves.

5   Make 12 rectangular mounds of rice, following the method on page 20. Instead of wrapping in nori, wrap 4 in lollo rosso leaves, 4 in butter lettuce and 4 in iceberg lettuce cups. Put 1–1½ tablespoons of haddock flakes on top of the rice in the lollo rosso leaves. Put 1–1½ tablespoons smoked salmon on the rice in the butter lettuce, and 1–1½ tablespoons caviar in the iceberg cups. Top the haddock with a little caviar, the salmon with a caperberry or caper and the caviar with a few flakes of haddock.

6   Arrange on a platter or small plates and serve with a small dish of soy sauce.

Battleship rolls can be made with lettuce leaves instead of nori. Use a lettuce with flexible leaves, such as butter lettuce or lollo rosso as ribbons and iceberg as cups.

lettuce rolls

Uramaki is an 'inside-out' roll, with nori inside and rice outside. This prawn tempura version is popular in restaurants – the nori prevents the vinegar in the rice and the oil in the tempura from touching each other. The unlikely combination of two opposing tastes makes a surprisingly delicious match.

inside-out sushi
uramaki

¾ quantity vinegared rice [page 11]
2 sheets nori seaweed
pickled ginger, to serve

Hand vinegar:
2 tablespoons Japanese rice vinegar
125 ml water

Tempura prawns:
8 large uncooked tiger prawn tails,
    4 peeled completely, 4 left with tail fins
    intact, deveined
100 g plain flour, sifted
4 tablespoons sesame seeds, black or white
salt
sunflower oil, for frying

8 cocktail sticks or bamboo skewers
a sushi rolling mat [makisu] covered with
    clingfilm

Makes 20 pieces [4 rolls]

1   Make the vinegared rice *[sumeshi]* following the method on page 11 and divide into 4. Mix the hand vinegar ingredients in a small bowl. Skewer a cocktail stick through each prawn from top to tail to prevent curling while cooking.

2   Cover one side of a sushi rolling mat *[makisu]* with clingfilm and put it on a dry cutting board, clingfilm side up.

3   Fill a wok or deep saucepan one-third full of oil and heat to 170°C [340°F] or until a cube of bread browns in about 60 seconds. To make the tempura batter, put 100 ml water in a bowl, sift the flour into the water and mix with a fork. One by one, dip the prawns in the batter, then fry in the hot oil for 3–4 minutes or until golden-brown. Remove and drain on kitchen paper and carefully remove and discard the cocktail sticks.

4   Put the nori on a completely dry cutting board. Dip your hands in the hand vinegar. Take a handful of the rice [2–3 heaped tablespoons] in your hands and make into a log shape. Put the rice in the centre of the nori. Using your fingers, spread it evenly all over, right to the edges. Sprinkle 1 tablespoon sesame seeds all over the rice.

5   Turn the whole thing over onto the clingfilm-covered mat.

6   Arrange 2 tempura prawns down the centre of the nori, with the tails sticking out at the ends [you can remove the tail fins if preferred].

7   Roll the mat following the method on page 14–15. Remove from the mat and repeat to make 3 more rolls, using black or white sesame seeds.

8   Cut each roll into 5 pieces and arrange on a platter. Serve with pickled ginger and a little soy sauce in a small dish beside the platter or in small individual plates.

A perfect sushi for parties. Serve the rice, nori sheets and prepared ingredients on plates and let people roll their own. Choose ingredients with varied tastes and colours. This is a delicious variation of the hand roll using smoked salmon instead of crabsticks.

smoked salmon hand rolls temaki

¾ **quantity vinegared rice**
  [page 11]
4 sheets nori seaweed
  or 8 salad leaves
pickled ginger, to serve

Hand roll fillings:
125 g smoked salmon
4 spring onions
6 cm pickled daikon
  [takuan]
1 avocado
juice of 1 lemon

Makes 8 rolls

1   Make the vinegared rice *[sumeshi]* following the method on page 11.

2   Cut the smoked salmon lengthways into 5 mm wide strips.

3   Finely slice the spring onions lengthways into 8–10 cm strips. Slice the pickled daikon thinly.

4   Cut the avocado in half, remove the stone and peel carefully. Thinly slice the flesh and brush with lemon juice.

5   Toast the nori sheets by quickly passing over a low flame to make them crisp and bring out the flavour. Cut each sheet in half crossways.

6   Put the rice in a serving bowl and arrange salmon, spring onion and avocado on a platter. Serve them on the table with the nori and pickled ginger in small separate plates .

7   To assemble, follow the step-by-step directions on the following page.

ASSEMBLING HAND ROLLS

2   Arrange your choice of fillings diagonally over
the rice from the centre to the outer corner.

1   Take one piece of nori seaweed in one hand and
add 2–3 tablespoons of vinegared rice *[sumeshi]*.
Spread the rice over one half of the nori.

3

4

3 Take the bottom right-hand corner and curl it towards the middle to form a cone.

4 Keep rolling the cone until complete. To glue the cone closed [optional], put a few grains of rice on the edge of the nori, and press together.

5 When the cone is complete, add your choice of a few drops of soy sauce, a few pieces of pickled ginger and a dab of wasabi paste.

5

Battera, a speciality from Osaka, is one of the most popular sushi in Japan. It is made in a container or moulded into a log with a sushi mat and cut into small pieces. In restaurants and shops it often comes wrapped up with a transparent sheet of kombu [dried kelp].

mackerel sushi pieces
battera

1 medium fresh mackerel, about 400 g, filleted
3–4 tablespoons Japanese rice vinegar
salt
½ quantity vinegared rice [page 11]

Hand vinegar:
2 tablespoons rice vinegar
125 ml water

To serve:
pickled ginger
Japanese soy sauce [shoyu]

a wooden mould or rectangular plastic container, 18 x 12 x 5 cm

Makes 1 battera [16 pieces]

1   Start the preparation for this dish a few hours before cooking the rice. Take a dish larger than the fish fillets and cover with a thick layer of salt. Put the mackerel fillets, flesh side down, on top of the salt and cover completely with more salt. Set aside for 3–4 hours. Remove mackerel and rub off the salt with damp kitchen paper. Carefully remove all the bones with tweezers, then put into a dish and pour the rice vinegar over the fillets. Leave to marinate for 30 minutes.

2   Make the vinegared rice *[sumeshi]* following the recipe on page 11. Mix the hand vinegar ingredients in a small bowl and set aside.

3   Using your fingers, carefully remove the transparent skin from each fillet, starting at the tail end. Put the fillets, skin side down, on a cutting board and slice off the highest part from the centre of the flesh so the the fillets will be fairly flat. Keep the trimmings.

4   Line a wet wooden mould or rectangular container with a large piece of clingfilm.

5   Put a fillet, skin side down, in the mould or container. Fill the gaps with the other fillet and trimmings. Dip your fingers in the hand vinegar, then press the cooked rice down firmly on top of the fish. Put the wet wooden lid on top, or fold in the clingfilm and put a piece of cardboard and a weight on top.

6   You can leave it in a cool place [not the refrigerator] for a few hours. When ready to serve, remove from the container and unwrap any clingfilm. Take a very sharp knife and wipe it with a vinegar-soaked cloth or piece of kitchen paper. Cut the block of sushi in 4 lengthways, then in 4 crossways, making 16 pieces in all.

7   Arrange on a plate, and serve with pickled ginger and a little soy sauce in small individual dishes.

PRESSED SUSHI

masu-zushi smoked fish sushi

Oshi-zushi [pressed sushi] like this, or *Bo-zushi* [log sushi] will keep for up to 36 hours — as a result, they are the best-selling items at all Japanese airports. Travellers buy them for Japanese friends living abroad as a reminder of the true taste of Japan. They are easy to make and can be made the day before.

1 Make the vinegared rice *[sumeshi]* following the method on page 11. Mix the hand vinegar ingredients in a small bowl and set aside.

2 Lay the smoked trout or salmon slices evenly in the bottom of a wet wooden mould. Alternatively, use a rectangular container lined with a piece of clingfilm large enough for the edges to hang out of the container.

3 Wet your hands in the hand vinegar, transfer the vinegared rice into the mould and press it firmly and evenly into the mould. Put the wet wooden lid on top. If using a plastic container, fold in the clingfilm to cover the rice and top with a piece cardboard just big enough to cover the rice, and put a weight on top. Leave in a cool place [but never the refrigerator] for 2–3 hours or overnight.

4 When ready to serve, remove from the container and unwrap any clingfilm. Take a very sharp knife and wipe it with a vinegar-soaked cloth or piece of kitchen paper. Cut the block of sushi into 4 lengthways, then in 4 crossways, making 16 pieces.

5 Arrange on a large serving plate. Put a fan-shaped piece of lemon on top. Serve with pickled ginger and a little Japanese soy sauce.

½ **quantity vinegared rice [page 11]**

Hand vinegar:
2 tablespoons Japanese rice vinegar
125 ml water

Toppings:
150 g smoked rainbow trout or smoked salmon, thickly sliced
2 slices lemon, cut into 16 fan-shaped pieces

To serve:
pickled ginger
Japanese soy sauce *[shoyu]*

a wooden mould or rectangular plastic container, 18 x 12 x 5 cm

Makes 1 block [16 pieces]

1   Make the vinegared rice *[sumeshi]* following the method on page 11.

2   Put the fish in a saucepan, add just enough boiling water to cover and simmer until well cooked. Drain, then carefully remove all the small bones. Pat dry with kitchen paper and put into the dry saucepan. Using a fork, crush into fine flakes. Add the sugar and a pinch of salt, then cook over a low heat, continuously stirring with a fork, for about 2 minutes, or until the fish is very dry and flaky. If using food colouring, dilute 1 drop with 1 tablespoon water, then stir quickly through the fish to spread the colour evenly. Remove from the heat and let cool. [Alternatively, use fresh salmon cooked to flakes in the same way or crush canned cooked red salmon into flakes.]

3   Bring a small saucepan of lightly salted water to the boil, add the peas and cook for 5 minutes or until soft. Drain and pat dry with kitchen paper. Crush with a mortar and pestle or in a food processor to form a smooth green paste. Stir in the sugar and a pinch of salt.

4   Lightly oil a small saucepan and heat over a moderate heat. Put the eggs, milk and sugar in a bowl, mix, then pour into the pan. Quickly stir with a fork to make soft scrambled eggs. Remove from the heat and let cool.

5   Divide the vinegared rice into three. To make the cherry blossom sushi, put 1 tablespoon of the pink fish flakes in the bottom of a small heart-shaped mould and press about 1 tablespoon of the rice on top. Turn out onto a plate, fish side up. Repeat until all the pink flakes and a third of the rice are used. Using a second mould, repeat using the green pea paste and another third of the rice. Using a third mould, repeat using the scrambled eggs with the remaining third of the rice. If using grilled fresh salmon, use a fourth mould.

6   Arrange cherry blossom, flower, star and spring green sushi on a large serving plate.

½ quantity vinegared rice [page 11]

Cherry blossom sushi:
100 g cod or haddock fillet, skinned
2 tablespoons sugar
salt and pepper
red vegetable food colouring*

Spring green sushi:
100 g shelled green peas
2 teaspoons sugar
salt

Golden star sushi:
2 eggs, beaten
1 tablespoon milk
1 tablespoon sugar

*star, daisy and diamond or heart shaped
   sushi moulds, or cookie cutters*

Makes 18-20 pieces

* If you don't want to use food colouring,
use grilled fresh salmon, flaked, instead
of the white fish and colouring.

stars, hearts and flowers

Just like cookies, these children's sushi are made in pretty colours and shapes. Specially shaped moulds are sold in Japanese stores, but if you don't have access to such exciting shops, use decorative cookie cutters and other mould shapes.

children's favourites

¾ quantity vinegared rice
[page 11]
3 sheets nori seaweed
Japanese soy sauce
[shoyu], to serve

Hand vinegar:
4 tablespoons Japanese
rice vinegar
250 ml water

Fillings:
1 egg, beaten
2 tablespoons sugar
6 cm carrot, sliced
lengthways into
5 mm sticks
2 thin frankfurters, 18 cm
long, or 4 Vienna
sausages, 9 cm long
6 cm cucumber
75 g canned red salmon,
drained
1 tablespoon mayonnaise
salt
sunflower oil, for frying

a Japanese omelette pan
or 20 cm non-stick
frying pan
a sushi rolling mat
[makisu]

Makes 6 rolls
[36 pieces].

'Sushi is fun when you make it for or with children. Devising sushi for non-Japanese kids led me to a surprise discovery of a match such as sausages and fish fingers with vinegared rice. Let's start with simple 'sausage rolls'.

1   Make vinegared rice following the method on page 11. Mix the hand vinegar ingredients in a bowl.

2   Strain the egg into a small bowl, add ½ tablespoon sugar and a pinch of salt and beat until dissolved. Heat a frying pan, brush with sunflower oil and rub off any excess with kitchen paper.

3   Pour in the egg mixture and spread evenly by tilting the pan to make a thin pancake. Prick any bubbles with a fork and fill any holes with egg by tilting the pan. After 30 seconds, turn the omelette over for 30 seconds to dry the other side and make it golden yellow. Remove from the heat, remove with a spatula, put on a cutting board and cut in half.

4   Blanch the carrot in about 250 ml boiling salted water at a high heat for 2–3 minutes. Lower the heat and then stir in 1½ tablespoons sugar and a pinch of salt. Simmer gently for another 2–3 minutes, then remove from the heat and let cool in the juice.

5   Put half the omelette on a board with the cut side nearest you and put a row of carrot strips beside the cut edge. Roll up the omelette tightly and secure the end with a cocktail stick. Repeat to make a second roll.

6   Cook the sausages according to the packet instructions and drain well on kitchen paper. Cut into 1 cm square sticks. Thickly peel the cucumber and finely shred the skin.

7   Put the canned salmon in a bowl, add the mayonnaise and pinch of salt and stir well.

8   Following the method on page 14, make 2 sushi rolls with a carrot-and-egg roll filling [remove the cocktail sticks first], 2 rolls with 1 frankfurter or 2 Vienna sausages in a row and 2 with salmon paste and cucumber shreds.

9   Cut each roll into 6 pieces and serve on a platter with separate dishes of Japanese soy sauce.

Hand moulding of rice is rather a messy job and it's also difficult to make identical shapes and sizes. I have come up with a simple solution, using an egg cup as a mould. These sushi are very easy to make, pretty to serve and delicious to eat.

egg cup sushi

¼ quantity vinegared rice [page 11]
5–6 smoked salmon slices, about 125 g, halved to make 10–12 pieces
lemon or lime wedges, to serve

Hand vinegar:
4 tablespoons Japanese rice vinegar
250 ml water

a small egg cup

Makes 10–12 pieces

1   Make the vinegared rice *[sumeshi]* following the method on page 11. Mix the hand vinegar ingredients in a small bowl and set aside.

2   Line an egg cup with clingfilm so it hangs over the edge of the cup. Line the whole cup with a piece of smoked salmon, filling any gaps with small pieces of salmon. Put 1 tablespoon of vinegared rice in the cup and press down gently with your thumbs. Do not over-fill. Trim the excess salmon from the rim. Lift up the clingfilm and turn out the moulded sushi, upside down, onto a plate. Repeat to make 10 pieces.

3   Arrange on a serving platter, add lemon or lime wedges and serve.

Variation:
Make soft scrambled eggs, using 2 eggs, 1 teaspoon sugar and a pinch of salt. Let cool. Lay a piece of clingfilm in the egg cup. Put 1 teaspoon of the scrambled eggs on the bottom. Gently press to make a firm base – the egg should come about half way up the side of the cup. Put 1 tablespoon of vinegared rice on top of the egg and again gently press down with your thumbs. Do not over-fill. Using the clingfilm, turn out the moulded sushi, upside down, onto a plate. Repeat this process for the remainder of the egg and rice. Serve with a tiny bit of red caviar on top.

An *inari* is a shrine dedicated to agriculture and the fox is regarded as the envoy of the god. People used to offer *abura-age* [fried bean curd] to the fox; hence this special name. This sushi makes an ideal picnic lunch and children's snack.

tofu bags inari-zushi

½ quantity vinegared rice [page 11]
3 fresh Japanese fried bean curd
  [abura-age]
200 ml chicken stock
3 tablespoons sugar
2 tablespoons mirin or sweet sherry
2 tablespoons Japanese soy sauce [shoyu]
2 dried shiitake [mushrooms]
5 cm carrot, finely chopped
1 tablespoon sake [optional]

To serve:
pickled ginger
Japanese soy sauce [shoyu]

Makes 6 tofu bags

1　Make the vinegared rice [sumeshi] following the method on page 11.

2　Put the fried bean curd [abura-age] on a cutting board and roll each one with a rolling pin. This separates the thin layers inside the bean curd, making a bag. Put the bean curd in a mixing bowl, pour over boiling water, then drain – this will reduce the oiliness.

3　Cut each piece in half and carefully open each piece from the cut side [if not opened already], to make a bag.

4　Put the chicken stock or water in a saucepan, add 2 tablespoons of the sugar and bring to the boil. Add the bean curd bags, cook 3 minutes on moderate heat, then add 1 tablespoon mirin and 1 tablespoon soy sauce. Simmer over a low heat for about 10 minutes until all the liquid disappears. Remove from the heat and transfer to a plate.

5　Meanwhile, soak the dried shiitake in a bowl of warm water for at least 30 minutes, then drain, reserving the liquid. Cut off the stems and finely chop the caps. Pour 50 ml of the soaking liquid into a saucepan, add the remaining sugar, mirin, soy sauce and sake and bring to the boil. Add the carrot and shiitake and simmer for 3–4 minutes until almost all the liquid is absorbed. Remove from the heat and let cool.

6　While the rice is still warm, fold in the cooked carrot and shiitake. Dip your hands in the hand vinegar and divide the rice mixture into 6 balls. Squeeze out excess juice from the bean curd bags and open with your fingers. Stuff a ball of rice into each bag and fold in the edge [optional]. You may cut some bags in half and stuff rice in the corner to make a three-cornered 'Napoleon's hat' shape.

7　Arrange the bags on a serving plate and serve with pickled ginger and soy sauce.

SUSHI BAGS

½ quantity vinegared rice [page 11]
10 eggs, beaten
2 tablespoons sugar
½ teaspoon sea salt
1 teaspoon cornflour blended with
    1 teaspoon water
2 tablespoons sesame seeds [black or white]
50 g anchovy fillets, finely chopped
1 bunch of mitzuna [optional]
sunflower oil, for frying

To serve:
pickled ginger
Japanese soy sauce [shoyu]

a 20 cm non-stick frying pan

Makes 8

1   Make the vinegared rice [sumeshi] following the method on page 11.

2   Put the eggs in a large mixing bowl and lightly beat with a fork. Strain through a sieve into another bowl. Add the sugar, salt and blended cornflour and mix well until dissolved. Do not whip.

3   Heat the frying pan, add a little oil and spread over the base with kitchen paper. Add 1 small ladle of the egg mixture and spread evenly over the base by tilting the pan. Cook over a low heat for about 30 seconds on each side until it becomes firm but not browned. Transfer to a plate and let cool. Repeat to make 8 egg pancakes.

4   Put the sesame seeds in a small saucepan and toss over a moderate heat until they start to pop. Remove from the heat and coarsely crush with a mortar and pestle.

5   While the rice is still warm, fold in the chopped anchovy fillets and crushed sesame seeds. Dip your hands in the hand vinegar, then divide the rice mixture into 8 balls.

6   Put an egg pancake on a board and put a rice ball in the centre. Fold the front of the pancake over the rice, then fold over the two sides, then the far side, like an envelope. Tuck the edges into the sides. Repeat to make 8 parcels. Alternatively, fold into a money bag, as shown [inset].

7   If using mitzuna herb to tie the parcels, soak the stems in boiling water for about 30 seconds, using 2 pieces per parcel. Serve with pickled ginger and soy sauce.

A fukusa is an elaborate napkin used for the traditional Japanese tea ceremony. It is folded in various ways and is an important part of the classic performance. It has lent its name to this folded pancake sushi.

omelette parcel sushi
fukusa-zushi

2 medium squid, cleaned
3 tablespoons sake
2–3 tablespoons Japanese
    rice vinegar
2 tablespoons sugar
1 tablespoon mirin or
    sweet sherry
2 tablespoons Japanese soy
    sauce *[shoyu]*
50 g minced chicken
    or beef
2 cm fresh ginger, peeled
    and finely chopped
⅔ quantity vinegared rice
    [page 11]
pickled ginger, to serve

Makes 10–12
    pieces

1   Peel the outer skin off the squid. It comes off easily if you hold the two flaps together and peel down the body. Put the 2 main bodies in a saucepan, add 1 tablespoon sake, cover with boiling water and simmer for 1–2 minutes. Do not overcook. Drain, rub the surface with a damp cloth to remove any marks, then sprinkle with the rice vinegar all over to retain the whiteness. Chop the flaps and tentacles.

2   Put the remaining sake, the sugar, mirin and soy sauce in a saucepan, mix and bring to the boil over moderate heat. Add the minced chicken or beef, the chopped squid flaps and tentacles and the chopped ginger, then stir vigorously with a fork until the meat turns white. Using a slotted spoon, transfer the cooked meat to another bowl, leaving the juice in the saucepan. Boil the juice over high heat for 1–2 minutes until thickened. Stir the meat back into the saucepan to absorb the juice and remove from heat.

3   Make the vinegared rice *[sumeshi]* following the method on page 11, and while still warm fold in the dry-cooked meat. Tightly stuff each squid body with half the rice mixture and, using a sharp knife, slice crossways into 5–6 pieces.

4   Arrange on plates and serve with pickled ginger.

stuffed squid sushi ika-zushi

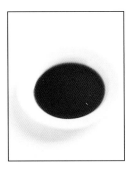

Meat is rarely used in sushi but this sweet, dry-cooked minced meat goes well with vinegared rice. It can be eaten as it is, or use it as a stuffing for squid and serve as an unusual party canapé. If you don't like to use meat, just use the squid flaps and tentacles in the *sumeshi* mixture, but reduce the cooking juice accordingly.

hand-moulded
sushi nigiri

Hand-moulded or *nigiri-zushi* is the king of all sushi. Though it looks simple, it is actually the most difficult to make and is not usually made at home, even in Japan.

⅓ quantity vinegared rice [page 11]

Hand vinegar:
4 tablespoons Japanese rice vinegar
250 ml water

Toppings:
2 uncooked tiger prawn tails
1 fillet fresh tuna or salmon,
    about 100 g, skinned
1 fillet fresh sea bream, about 100 g, skinned
100 g squid, cleaned and skinned
2 eggs, beaten
2 tablespoons dashi stock
1 teaspoon mirin or sweet sherry
1 teaspoon Japanese soy sauce *[shoyu]*
2 teaspoons wasabi paste or powder
2 shiso leaves or basil leaves
a small piece of nori seaweed,
    cut into 5 mm strips
salt

To serve:
pickled ginger, to serve
Japanese soy sauce *[shoyu]*

a sushi rolling mat [makisu]

Makes 8-10 pieces

1   Make the vinegared rice *[sumeshi]* following the method on page 11. Mix the hand vinegar ingredients in a small bowl and set aside.

2   Skewer a cocktail stick through each prawn from top to tail to prevent curling while cooking. Blanch in boiling water for 2 minutes until lightly cooked and pink. Drain and put under running water. Remove and discard the cocktail sticks, shells and back vein. Make a slit up the belly lengthways and open out.

3   Slice the tuna or salmon and sea bream into rectangular pieces, 7 x 3 x 1 cm thick. Cut the squid into similar rectangular pieces, and make fine slits on one side of each piece to make the squid more tender.

4   Using the beaten eggs, chicken stock, mirin and soy sauce, make an omelette following the method on page 60. Put the rolled omelette on a sushi rolling mat and tightly roll into a flat rectangular shape. When cool, cut 2 rectangular pieces, 7 x 3 x 1 cm thick.

5   If using wasabi powder, mix with 2 teaspoons water in an egg cup and stir well to make a clay-like consistency. Leave upside down to prevent drying.

6   Wet your hands in the hand vinegar mixture, take a handful [about 1–2 tablespoons] of the cooked rice in one hand and mould into a rectangular cylinder about 5 x 2 x 2 cm. Put a tiny bit of wasabi on top and cover with an opened prawn.

7   Repeat, making 2 nigiri topped with prawns, 2 with tuna or salmon, 2 with sea bream, 2 with squid on top of a shiso leaf and 2 with omelette. When assembling the nigiri with omelette, do not add wasabi: instead, tie with a thin nori ribbon, about 5 mm wide.

8   Arrange on a platter and serve with pickled ginger and Japanese soy sauce in a small dish. Alternatively, serve as party canapés or on small plates as part of a meal.

As an alternative, serve the nigiri in lettuce 'boats'. They look very pretty and are also easier to pick up and eat – important at a party.

lettuce boats

½ quantity vinegared rice [page 11]

Hand vinegar:
4 tablespoons Japanese rice vinegar
250 ml water

Toppings:
100 g beef fillet, about 7 cm thick
vegetable oil, for rubbing
1–2 rollmops [marinated Bismarck herring]
8 asparagus tips
2 teaspoons wasabi paste or powder
4 Little Gem lettuce leaves
8 small chicory [witloof] leaves

To serve:
sprigs of cress or shredded spring onions
a small strip of nori seaweed
1 spring onion, finely chopped
2.5 cm fresh ginger, peeled and grated
2 tablespoons white wine
1½ tablespoons Japanese soy sauce [shoyu]
juice of ½ lemon

Makes 12

1   Make the vinegared rice [sumeshi] following the method on page 11. Mix the hand vinegar ingredients in a small bowl and set aside.

2   Rub the beef all over with vegetable oil. Grill at a high heat until golden-brown on all sides, but rare in the middle. Plunge into iced water to stop the cooking. Remove from the water, pat dry with kitchen paper and cut 4 thin slices, about 7 x 4 cm. All the slices should be red inside and brown around the edges.

3   Cut the rollmops into 4 and make a little lengthways slit in the skin of each piece.

4   Cook the asparagus in lightly salted water for 5 minutes until soft. Drain and place under running water to arrest cooking and bring out the colour. Pat dry with kitchen paper.

5   If using wasabi powder, mix with 2 teaspoons water in an egg cup, stir to make a clay-like consistency, then turn upside down to stop it drying out.

6   Dip your hands in the hand vinegar and take a handful of the cooked rice in one hand [about 1–2 tablespoons]. Mould it into a rectangular shape about 5 x 2 x 2 cm. Repeat with the remaining rice, making 12 portions. Put a tiny dab of wasabi on top of 4 portions.

7   Arrange a slice of beef on 1 portion of wasabi-and-rice, with the two short sides hanging over the end. Top with a few sprigs of cress. Repeat with the other 3 slices of beef and set them in 4 Little Gem lettuce leaves.

8   Arrange 2 asparagus tips on another rice portion and tie with a nori ribbon. Repeat to make 3 more. Arrange a piece of rollmop on each of the remaining 4 rice portions and insert chopped spring onion and grated ginger into the slits. Arrange all the leaf boats on a serving platter. Mix the white wine, soy sauce and the lemon juice in a small bowl. Serve the lettuce boats with a small bowl of lemon sauce and another of plain soy sauce.

Gomoku-zushi means '5-kinds sushi' and usually has 5–8 ingredients. This standard mixture is a popular luncheon dish because it's easy to cook and to adjust the volume and produces a relaxed atmosphere.

lunchbox sushi mixture

1 quantity vinegared rice [page 11]

Toppings:
3–4 dried shiitake [mushrooms]
6 tablespoons sugar
3 tablespoons Japanese soy sauce [*shoyu*]
½ carrot, finely sliced into 2 cm strips
200 ml chicken stock or water
1 tablespoon sake
50 g green beans, trimmed
½ small lotus root [*renkon*] [optional]
200 ml rice vinegar
2 eggs, beaten
salt
sunflower oil, for frying

Serves 4–6

1   Soak the shiitake in warm water for 30 minutes. Drain, retaining the soaking liquid. Remove and discard the stems, then thinly slice the caps. Put in a small saucepan, cover with 100 ml soaking liquid, 2 tablespoons sugar and 2 tablespoons soy sauce. Simmer for 10 minutes or until most of the liquid disappears. Transfer to a bowl and let cool.

2   Put the carrot in the saucepan with water to cover. Bring to the boil, then drain in a colander. Put the chicken stock or water in the saucepan, add the remaining soy sauce and sake, bring to the boil, add the carrot and cook for 3–4 minutes. Transfer to a bowl and let cool.

3   Add some lightly salted water to the saucepan, bring to the boil, add the beans and boil for 2 minutes until just soft. Drain and cool under running water. Pat dry with kitchen paper and slice diagonally into 5 cm long shreds.

4   Peel the lotus root, if using, and slice into thin rings. Bring the small saucepan of water to the boil, add 1 tablespoon rice vinegar and the lotus root and boil until just soft. Drain and transfer to a mixing bowl. Put the remaining rice vinegar in the saucepan, add the remaining sugar and 2 teaspoons salt, bring to the boil and stir until dissolved. Remove from the heat, add to the lotus root and let marinate for 15–20 minutes.

5   Beat the eggs with a pinch of salt. Heat a 20 cm frying pan, brush with sunflower oil, add the egg and cook until just set. Transfer the egg pancake to a cutting board and cut into fine shreds, 5 cm long.

6   Make the vinegared rice *[sumeshi]* following the recipe on page 11. Put the rice in a bowl and fold in all the ingredients except the egg shreds and a few of the beans. Transfer to bowls or lunchboxes, top with the egg shreds and beans and serve.

½ quantity vinegared rice
[page 11]

Sashimi (your choice of):
**2 uncooked tiger prawns,
peeled but with tail fins
intact**
1 octopus tentacle
**125 g fresh tuna and/or
salmon**
1 turbot fillet, about 75 g
**1 small squid, cleaned and
skinned**
**2 large dried shiitake
[mushrooms]**
1 teaspoon sugar
1 teaspoon mirin [rice wine]
salt

To serve:
4 cm cucumber
pink pickled ginger
wasabi paste
Japanese soy sauce [shoyu]

Serves 2

1   Make the vinegared rice [*sumeshi*] following the method on page 11.

2   Bring a saucepan of lightly salted water to the boil, add the prawns and poach for 1–2 minutes until just pink. Remove with a slotted spoon, cool under running water, then pat dry with kitchen paper.

3   Return the pan of water to the boil, add the octopus tentacle and cook for 7–8 minutes. Drain and cool under running water. Pat dry with kitchen paper and slice diagonally into thin discs.

4   Cut the fish into 4 slices each.

5   Put the squid, skin side up, on a cutting board and make very fine slits two-thirds of the way through the thickness, first lengthways, then crossways. Put in a bowl, pour over boiling water and drain. As the squid curls up, the slits open to form a flower. Immediately plunge into cold water. Pat dry with kitchen paper and cut into 4 bite size pieces.

6   Soak the shiitake in warm water for 30 minutes and drain, retaining the soaking liquid. Cut off the stems and put in a saucepan with the sugar, mirin and a pinch of salt. Cover with some of the soaking liquid, stir, then bring to the boil and simmer for 4–5 minutes until most of the liquid disappears. Let cool in the liquid.

7   Cut 2 green slices off the cucumber, 5 cm wide. Make fine slits lengthways, leaving 1 cm intact on one side. Open up the slits to make 2 cucumber fans.

8   Divide the rice between 2 bowls and arrange the seafood over the rice and top with a cucumber fan and a pile of pink pickled ginger. Serve on small individual plates with a tiny heap of wasabi, and a little jug of soy sauce.

sushi in a bowl edomae chirashi-zushi

A bowl of sushi with sashimi on top is a favourite in Tokyo. You can use just one ingredient like tuna, or the assorted sashimi normally used in restaurants including tuna, prawn, eel, sea bass, shellfish, herring roe, salmon roe – almost any good material from the market on the day. My selection is good for serving at home.

This is a pretty, modern variation of *chirashi-zushi* decorated with 'petals' made of radish and egg - ideal for the Girls' Day Festival, which falls on 3rd March in Japan, or any spring gathering.

1 quantity vinegared rice [page 11]

Radish petals:
4–5 radishes, trimmed
2 tablespoons rice vinegar
2 tablespoons sugar

Egg petals:
1 egg, beaten
¼ teaspoon cornflour mixed with a little water
sunflower oil, for frying

Your choice of:
5 dried shiitake [mushrooms]
5 tablespoons sugar
2½ tablespoons mirin [rice wine]
1 teaspoon Japanese soy sauce [*shoyu*]
50 ml chicken stock
½ carrot, sliced into 2–3 cm matchsticks
25 g mangetout [snowpeas], trimmed
75 g cod fillet
1 tablespoon sake
red vegetable food colouring [optional]
3 tablespoons white sesame seeds, lightly toasted in a dry frying pan
200 g small prawns, peeled and lightly cooked
salt

flower cutters or a small sharp knife

Serves 4–6

tub of spring sushi

1 Make the vinegared rice [*sumeshi*] following the method on page 11.

2 Cut a wedge out of each radish, then slice each radish crossways to form 5–6 petal shapes. Put the rice vinegar and sugar in a bowl and stir well until sugar has dissolved. Add the radish slices and marinate for a few hours or overnight. The red colour dissolves into the vinegar, making the slices cherry pink.

3 Mix the egg in a bowl with a pinch of salt and the blended cornflour. Heat a small frying pan, brush with sunflower oil, add the egg mixture and cook until set. Using moulds or a small knife, cut out small shapes from the egg pancake such as hearts or petals.

4 Soak the shiitake in warm water for 30 minutes, then drain, retaining the soaking liquid. Discard the stems and thinly slice the caps crossways. Put the shiitake slices, 100 ml from the soaking liquid and 2 tablespoons of the sugar in a saucepan, bring to the boil and cook for 3–4 minutes. Add the mirin and soy sauce, then simmer until the liquid disappears.

5 Put the chicken stock in a saucepan, add ½ teaspoon of the sugar, a pinch of salt, and the carrot. Bring to the boil and cook for 2–3 minutes until just soft. Let cool in the juice.

6 Blanch the mangetout in lightly salted water. Slice diagonally into diamonds.

7 Bring a saucepan of water to the boil, add the cod, simmer for 3–4 minutes, then drain. Carefully remove the skin and all the bones. Return to a dry saucepan, add 1 tablespoon sake, the remaining sugar and a pinch of salt. Finely flake over a low heat, using a fork. If using red colouring, dilute it in a little water, then quickly stir to make a light pink *soboro* [fish flakes].

8 While the rice is still warm, fold in the shiitake, carrot matchsticks, flaked fish, prawns and sesame seeds. Top with the radish and egg 'petals' and serve.

Freshness of the fish is an absolute requirement for sashimi. So, arrange with your fishmonger that the fish you are buying are fresh in on the day. Trendy fishmongers even fillet fish for sashimi for you but it's best if you do it yourself just before serving.

classic sashimi

1 sea bream fillet
1 small fresh mackerel
1 slice of lemon, cut into 8 fan-shaped wedges
150 g tuna
150 g salmon fillet
1 small squid, cleaned and skinned
5 cm large daikon [white radish], peeled
4 shiso leaves [optional]

To serve:
4 teaspoons wasabi paste or powder [page 62]
Japanese soy sauce [shoyu]

Serves 4

1   Put the sea bream fillet on a cutting board, skin side down. Hold down the skin of the tail with your fingers, then run the blade along the skin, separating the flesh. Cut the whole fillet lengthways along the centre line. Insert the blade diagonally against the cutting board and slice each fillet crossways into 8 pieces, 1 cm thick. Make a slit in each piece and insert a fan-shaped piece of lemon.

2   Salt and vinegar the mackerel following the method on page 30. Slice the fillets into 1 cm pieces, as above.

3   Slice the tuna and salmon into 8 pieces, 6 x 3 cm, about 1 cm thick.

4   Cut the squid into 8 pieces and finely slice each piece lengthways, leaving the pieces attached at one end.

5   Using a mandoline or sharp knife, finely shred the daikon. Put the shreds in a bowl of iced water for about 30 minutes to make them crisp. Drain and pat dry with kitchen paper.

6   To serve, put a mound of daikon shreds, a small mound of wasabi paste and a shiso leaf, if using, on each plate. Add 2 slices of each fish and serve with a small dish of Japanese soy sauce.

SASHIMI
RECIPES

seared tuna
sashimi salad

You may take some time to get used to the idea of eating completely raw fish, but lightly blanched or seared fillet with salad is a good starting point. You can use other fish such as turbot, salmon or swordfish.

200 g fresh tuna or swordfish, skinned
green salad leaves
a small clump of enoki mushrooms, trimmed and separated

Wasabi dressing:
juice of 1 lemon
2 teaspoons wasabi paste
1½ tablespoons Japanese soy sauce [*shoyu*]

Serves 4

1   Grill the tuna or swordfish at a high heat for about 1 minute on each side until the surfaces are seared but the inside is still raw. Plunge into iced water. Drain and pat dry with kitchen paper. Slice into 5 mm thick pieces.

2   Mix the lemon juice, wasabi and soy sauce in a small bowl and set aside.

3   Arrange the salad leaves and enoki mushrooms in the centre of a large serving plate and arrange the seared fish over the leaves. Just before serving, pour the wasabi dressing over the top.

japanese omelette
tamago yaki

This is the basic method for cooking Japanese omelette. It is a regular breakfast item as well as being used for sushi.

4 eggs
1 egg yolk
2½ tablespoons sugar
1 teaspoon Japanese soy sauce [*shoyu*]
salt
1–2 tablespoons sunflower oil

*1 Japanese omelette pan or
    20 cm non-stick frying pan*
hashi [chopsticks] or fork

Makes 1 omelette

1   Using a fork, beat the eggs and egg yolk and strain through a sieve into a bowl. Add the sugar, soy sauce and pinch of salt and stir well until the sugar has dissolved. Do not whisk or make bubbles.

2   Heat a Japanese omelette pan or frying pan over moderate heat and add a little oil. Spread evenly over the base by tilting the pan, then wipe off excess oil with kitchen paper, at the same time making sure the surface is absolutely smooth. Keep the oiled paper on a plate.

3   Lower the heat and pour one-third of the egg mixture evenly over the base by tilting the pan. If large air bubbles pop up immediately, the pan may be too hot – then remove the pan from the heat and put it back on when the egg starts to set.

4   Prick any air bubbles with a fork and when the egg is about to set, using chopsticks or a fork, roll the egg layer 2–3 times from one side to the other. Oil the empty base of the pan with the oiled paper and push the rolled egg back to the other side.

5   Again using the oiled paper, brush the base of the pan, then pour half the remaining egg mixture evenly over the base by tilting the pan and lifting the egg roll so the egg mixture flows underneath.

6   When the egg starts to set, roll again, using the first roll as the core. Repeat this oiling and rolling using up the remaining egg mixture. Remove from the pan and let cool before cutting.

BASIC
RECIPES

wasabi - japanese horseradish

Freshly grated wasabi root, available in Japan, is divine. However ready-made wasabi pastes are now so good that many restaurants, even in Japan, use them rather than labouring to grate fresh ones. Pastes are sold in tubes, and powder in cans. Tubes are handy to use but freshly made paste from powder has more kick and better flavour.

1   Put 1 teaspoon of wasabi powder in an egg cup and add 1 teaspoon of water. Stir vigorously with a teaspoon to make a clay-like consistency. Turn the egg cup upside-down to keep the wasabi moist until serving.

Makes enough for 10 pieces rolled sushi

pickled ginger

1 teaspoon salt
100 g fresh ginger, peeled
100 ml rice vinegar
1¼ tablespoons sugar

Makes about 350 ml

Gari — sushi shop jargon for pickled ginger slices — is always served with sushi and sashimi. It is delicious to eat and also works as a mouth freshener.

1   Rub the salt into the ginger and leave overnight. Drain and wipe with kitchen paper.

2   Mix the rice vinegar, sugar and 3½ tablespoons water in a mixing bowl. Stir until dissolved, add the ginger and set aside to marinate for 1 week. Alternatively, finely slice the ginger, blanch for 2 minutes, then marinate as before. It is ready to use when it turns slightly pink. Store in an airtight container in the fridge — it keeps for several months.

3   To serve, remove from the marinade and slice very thinly along the grain.

DIRECTORY

ATARIYA FOODS

• Main Shop
595 High Road,
West Finchley,
London N12 0DY
Tel 020 8446 6669
Tuesday to Sunday 10am–7pm

• West Acton Branch
7 Station Parade,
Noel Road,
London W3 0DS
Tel 020 8896 1552
Tuesday to Friday 10am–6.30pm
Saturday and Sunday 10am–7pm

BARIGATO

48–50 Brewer Street,
London
Tel 020 7287 1722
Monday to Saturday 9.30am–9.30pm
Sunday 11am–8pm

INTEL

126 Malden Road,
New Malden, Surrey KT3 6DD
Tel 020 8942 9552
Fax 020 8949 7617
Limited mail order available
Daily 9.30am–7pm

KIRIN BREWERY

The Eagle Brewery,
Havelock Street,
Bedford MK40 4LU
Tel 01234 272766
Fax 01234 279001
(for Japanese beer only)
Monday to Friday 9am–5pm

MIURA FOODS

• Main Shop
44 Coombe Road,
Norbiton, Nr Kingston,
Surrey KT2 7AE
Tel 020–8549 8076
• Croydon Branch
5 Limpsfield Road,
Sanderstead, Surrey CR2 9LA
Tel 020–8651 4498
Tuesday to Saturday 9am–6pm
Sunday 10am–6pm

NATURAL HOUSE

Japan Centre,
212 Piccadilly,
London W1V 9LD
Tel 020 7434 4218
Fax 020 7287 1082
Mail order available.
Monday to Saturday 10am–7.30pm
Sunday 11am–7pm

ORIENTAL CITY

399 Edgeware Road,
Colindale,
London NW9 0JJ
Tel 020 8200 0009
Monday to Saturday 10am–8pm
Sunday 10am–7pm
   (Supermarket 12noon–6pm)

T.K.TRADING

Unit 6/7, The Chase Centre,
Chase Road, North Acton,
London NW10 6QD
Tel 020 8453 1001
Fax 020 8453 0606
email tktrade@uk2.so-net.com
Mail order available
Daily 10am–5pm

INDEX